...and that is why we teach

A Celebration of Teachers

Follow your heart
Trust your intuition

Patti Graham

by Patti Graham
illustrations by Megan D. Wellman

FERNE PRESS

...and that is why we teach
Copyright © 2008 by Patti Graham
Illustrations by Megan D. Wellman
Printed in the United States of America

Summary: A book that celebrates all the unique qualities that make up a teacher.

Library of Congress Cataloging-in-Publication Data
Graham, Patti
...and that is why we teach / Patti Graham – First Edition
ISBN-13: 978-1-933916-23-1
1. Teachers 2. Inspiration 3. Education 4. Children 5. Elementary students
6. Middle school students 7. High school students
I. Graham, Patti II. Title ...and that is why we teach
Library of Congress Control Number: 2008922629

FERNE PRESS

Ferne Press is an imprint of Nelson Publishing & Marketing
366 Welch Road, Northville, MI 48167
www.nelsonpublishingandmarketing.com
(248) 735-0418

Dedication

To my mother and father, Robert and Betty Tontalo, who face every day with generosity, compassion, and courage.

To my husband, Dennis Graham, my best friend and source of strength.

With special thanks...

to Megan Wellman for her whimsical, enchanting illustrations.

to Marian Nelson for creating a dynamic, collaborative team.

to Kris Yankee and Kathy Hiatt for their insightful suggestions.

to Dr. Wayne W. Dyer, whose message of living life on purpose helped me find my voice and understand that everyone we meet in life is a teacher.

and to all of my students, for allowing me to be a part of their lives.

In loving memory of Tony Sevakis, who passionately embraced life and touched the hearts of everyone he met. I know he would be so happy to see that this book has come to life at last.

Think back.
Who was *your* favorite teacher?
We all have one.
And, even after all these years,
you can *still* remember that smile,
the twinkling eyes.
There was a special something about this remarkable teacher
who imprinted an indelible memory on your heart.

It probably isn't so much about
what they taught in the classroom that mattered.
It's more about the way they made you feel.
The way you were treated.
The way they *believed* in you,
maybe when nobody else did.
That might have *been* exactly the thing
that gave you hope
or confidence to take a chance,
and maybe even,
to believe in yourself.

Endlessly inspiring,
deeply kind,
worldly and wise,
glowing with an inner light,
a special teacher spoke to your heart.
You know the one.

What is it about a teacher
that can create such a profound impact
on the life of a child?

Teachers are leaders

Leading with passion and enthusiasm,
with strength of character
and kindness in spirit.

Leading with honesty and integrity.

Leading by example,
in every action, word, and deed.

Leading by modeling the ability
to laugh and learn from mistakes.

Teachers take the lead in their classrooms,
striving to help students find their voices,
to follow their dreams.

Charismatic teachers who lead with joy
set the tone each morning with their positive demeanor,
creating a jubilant climate
where students are awakened to possibilities.

Students respond instinctively to an optimistic approach,
freed to embrace their day with exuberance,
eager to learn.

Leading children safely outside for a fire drill
or leading them towards a life-long love of learning,
teachers unhesitatingly
lead from the heart.

Teachers are igniters

Teachers set off a chain reaction
of contagious positive energy.
It all begins with a vision:
to build an oasis,
a sanctuary,
a magical space,
where learning sparkles in the eyes of the children.

Joy vibrates in this room,
and everyone who enters can feel it.
Children are inspired here.
Families are valued here.
Colleagues are drawn inside.

It's as if the people, the books, the walls themselves
are humming the same lively tune.

Something wonderful happens in this kind of classroom
where the teacher envisions a stimulating center of learning
and transmits that excitement to students.

Ignited by the teacher's imagination
and fueled by the energy
of authentic and passionate learners,
education becomes a living thing,
a glowing radiance,
observed in the faces of students
within the walls of this welcoming wonderland.

Teachers are bridge builders and trailblazers

Exploring deep shadowy woods,
teachers carve trails,
post encouraging signs,
and build sturdy bridges across unfamiliar territories
so their students may move bravely
from the known to the unknown.

They encourage children to stop frequently along the way,
to notice the amazing wonders all around them,
and to be constantly aware of just how much there is
to see,
to touch,
to learn,
to know,
and to do.

With unhesitating confidence
in their ability
to embrace the challenges ahead,
teachers empower students
on their adventurous journey toward independence.

Together,
teachers and students celebrate
beginnings, middles, and endings
of the exciting process of discovery.

Children cartwheel over obstacles,
swing joyfully from one idea to another,
shout, laugh, and leap with abandon
as they reach the top of a difficult peak.

Teachers are listeners

Two ears, one mouth.
Teachers know it's in a child's best interest
to talk less and listen more.

Compassion comes from actively listening
not only with the ears,
but with eyes, heart, and soul.

Listening, really listening,
trusted teachers honor their students
with patient and meaningful moments of connection
in the midst of a busy day.

Teachers watch for clues a child may be leaving,
consciously or unconsciously.
They lean in closely, open their hearts,
set judgment aside,
and truly listen.

Teachers pay close attention to tiny signals:
a sad smile,
downcast eyes,
disheartened body language.
Teachers intuitively hear a child's message.

The silent, inner voice knowingly guides the teacher
to be a child's ally and advocate.

No matter how the message is communicated,
children trust that their teacher
will be looking out for them.

Listening with the volume turned all the way up,
teachers provide unconditional support to children
who are counting on a perceptive friend.

Teachers are team builders

The classroom team,
a unique blend of students and their teacher,
is a dynamic living organism that thrives
as all members unite
in acknowledgment, validation, and support
of one another.

In this synergistic, inclusive team,
one message is understood by all:
in working together,
each individual will go farther,
achieve more,
soar higher.

As respect and trust are cultivated,
friendships flourish.
Camaraderie enlivens the group.

Approaching challenges,
teammates rely on one another
to support and encourage.
They stand ready to catch one who might stumble
and urge them forward
in the right direction again.

Instilled within each member of this dynamic team
is the knowledge that as one succeeds,
everyone shares in the victory.
Spontaneous celebrations recognize accomplishments
and affirm team spirit.

Trust bonds the team together.
And everybody wins.

Teachers are gardeners

Blooming wonders, astonishing and *beautiful*,
vibrantly grow in classroom gardens
where teachers gently *sprinkle* in
just the right amount
of fertilizing nourishment.
They untangle the weeds,
watch out for pesky pests,
and provide a temporary scaffold
when a tender sprout needs someone to lean on.

Tending carefully to each fragile learner,
teachers observe transformations
in their little human *beans*!
They plant *seeds* of possibility,
knowing something wonderful will emerge.

Children need two important things to grow:
roots and wings!

Attentive teachers join hands with families
to carefully provide a rich and fertile landscape,
ensuring children are firmly grounded.
With this solid foundation,
children *begin* to *seek* the light
and reach for the *sky*.

The hope of tomorrow is growing today
in classroom gardens
as caretaking teachers rely
on a loving touch,
boundless hope,
and a very special kind of green thumb.

Teachers are climatologists

In this inviting place, students matter,
and they know it.

This is a safe space where imagination is nurtured,
where questions are welcomed,
where curious minds are awakened and expanded.

This radiant kingdom,
carefully designed with insight and understanding,
offers children the opportunity
to explore and experiment with life,
comfortably trying on the world for size.

Children investigate, reflect upon,
and discuss questions of the day,
often amazing adults with their surprising observations
and innocent wisdom.

Big concepts click, ideas come to life,
dreams float like bubbles
in a world where each child's best interests
are truly important.

Authentic writing and art of children,
prominently displayed around the classroom,
reinforce the importance of hard work,
purposeful effort, and perseverance.

Teachers create an enchanted learning climate within their rooms,
an exciting environment where inspiration bursts
and learning explodes like dazzling fireworks!

Teachers are travel guides

Standing nose to nose
with a curious three-toed sloth twirled around their waists,
students gaze into the eyes of the sweet, sleepy creature.
Their visit to the Costa Rican rain forest
will be remembered
with the sensation of embracing one
who is just trying to survive.

Climbing up steps
of the ancient, flat-topped pyramids
at Chitzen Itza, Mexico,
the class pushes upward,
higher and higher towards the sun,
just as the Mayans did thousands of years ago.
They wander in wonder
through the vast city,
once spectacular,
now only ruins.
They hear whispers on the wind,
ghostly storytellers
speaking of rituals and rain and quests for gold.

Diving into warm tropical Caribbean waters,
they stretch out and float,
looking down into the realm below.
The coral reef bursts into life.
A giant, green sea turtle paddles past.
Millions of colorful fish
zip, wiggle, and splash by.
Graceful sea fans wave,
and grand coral formations
turn the scene into an incredible undersea kingdom.

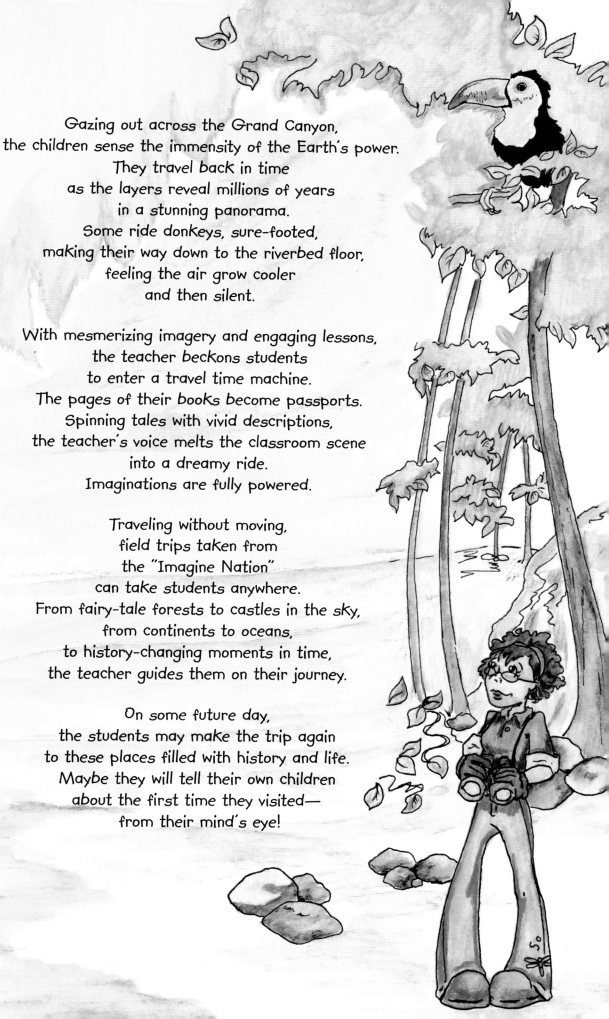

Gazing out across the Grand Canyon,
the children sense the immensity of the Earth's power.
They travel back in time
as the layers reveal millions of years
in a stunning panorama.
Some ride donkeys, sure-footed,
making their way down to the riverbed floor,
feeling the air grow cooler
and then silent.

With mesmerizing imagery and engaging lessons,
the teacher beckons students
to enter a travel time machine.
The pages of their books become passports.
Spinning tales with vivid descriptions,
the teacher's voice melts the classroom scene
into a dreamy ride.
Imaginations are fully powered.

Traveling without moving,
field trips taken from
the "Imagine Nation"
can take students anywhere.
From fairy-tale forests to castles in the sky,
from continents to oceans,
to history-changing moments in time,
the teacher guides them on their journey.

On some future day,
the students may make the trip again
to these places filled with history and life.
Maybe they will tell their own children
about the first time they visited—
from their mind's eye!

Teachers are healers

"Let the wild rumpus begin!"

Jubilant and playful,
rambunctious and noisy,
children enthusiastically celebrate being alive.

Flying off the bucking pony of a swing,
tumbling from skyscraping monkey bars,
or crashing, smack into a best friend's nose,
bumps and bruises can sometimes
bring the world to a screeching halt.

Teachers attend to the little boo-boos along the way
with calming words,
super-hero cartoon bandages,
and the mystical powers of a cool drink of water.

It seems teachers have a special kind of glue for broken places,
healing words for bruised egos,
and an unflinching resistance to yuckiness.

Often the presence of their caring teacher,
with a gentle squeeze of the hand
and a warm look in their eyes,
will be just the right prescription
for making it all better.

Curing the hiccups with a surprise "boo!"
or soothing a sore elbow with a dab of magic hand lotion,
teachers are compassionate caregivers
who nurture children with kindness and humor.

And if all else fails,
a handful of m&m's from the teacher's secret drawer
will often miraculously melt away any remaining tears.

Teachers are cheerleaders

Whether energetically cheering in the front of the stands,
shouting, "Yes, you can do it!"
or gently guiding at the side of one child,
whispering thoughtful, inspiring words,
teachers urge students
to move forward,
to take a chance,
to keep trying.

Passionate and positive,
teachers transmit powerful messages
that override a student's insecurities
and negative self-doubts.

Never giving up,
teachers reach out their hand to the struggling learner
with the intention of discovering hidden potential.
Caring teachers believe in their students,
lending strength to fragile spirits
learning to fly.

Students are transported to extraordinary heights
as motivational teachers applaud and encourage
their tentative steps
in the right direction.

More importantly,
as they reach their personal goals,
children begin to believe in themselves.
The cheering now comes from inside.

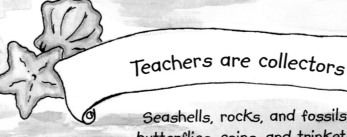

Teachers are collectors

Seashells, rocks, and fossils,
butterflies, coins, and trinkets,
tiny models of forts and castles,
vast book collections.

Stashed in every nook and cranny,
tucked away in basements, attics, and closets,
or displayed on classroom bookshelves,
collections of immense value
are located somewhere close to a teacher.

Collecting materials for sharing and examining,
teachers can't help themselves
from being on a never-ending search
for educational *stuff*.
Treasure collecting is essential to their being.
It's an avowed quest.

Displayed in the hands-on museum of a classroom,
colorful starfish, curvy pink conch shells, and tiny golden seahorses
bring the ocean to life
for students who live in places far from the sea.

Brightly colored Mexican blankets,
painted wooden shoes from Holland,
or a beautiful silk Japanese kimono
placed in the hands of children
personalizes the learning,
making it real.

Collections, unique, unusual, and thought-provoking,
help students visualize their expansive world.

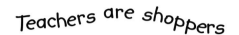

Teachers are shoppers

Teachers have a detective's nose
for discovering great buys and freebies.
Always on the lookout for special discounts and super sales,
teachers haul shopping bags and load their cars
with treasures for their classroom.

One hundred free cardboard cartons?
Yes, just the right size to make classroom mailboxes!
Crafty teachers fill up their trunks.
Notebooks for only ten cents each?
Wise shopping teachers buy four cases,
just in case students may be in need this year.
Mega sale on animal crackers, magic markers,
sidewalk chalk, or hand sanitizer?
Thrifty, pro-active teachers think ahead and stockpile.

Desks, chairs, textbooks on shelves?
These basic ingredients are provided in most classrooms.
But teachers are on the hunt
to find those special items that don't come standard.

Like birthday pencils, happy stickers,
the classroom library of books,
inspiring posters, puzzles, and games,
funny puppets, plants, and aquariums,
the friendly rocking chair.

These are touches that soften the edges
and send the message:
"Children are welcome here!"

Teachers are planet ambassadors

Peace among nations will become real
as individuals extend their hands in friendship
to someone of another
culture, race, or religion.
Without prejudice.
Without hesitation.

Teachers know this essential truth
and communicate it to students
through the consistent practice
of honoring and respecting all life.

Every day.
With every interaction.

As teachers model an all-inclusive world view,
demonstrating an open-minded
and caring approach,
children follow their guiding light.

Illuminating opportunities abound in classrooms
of rich multicultural diversity.
Unconcerned about differences,
children innocently smile and ask one another,
"Do you wanna play?"
It's natural.

As students live and learn together,
focusing on their similarities,
their feelings,
their dreams,
and their futures,
differences diminish.
These personal relationships are the foundation
for creating a more peaceful and harmonious planet.

"Be the change you wish to see in the world."
Gandhi's insights inspire
and present a challenge to all generations,
but especially the young.

Change begins with one.
One friendship,
one classroom,
one world.

Peace begins with a smile.

Teachers are facilitators

Teachers don't need to control every single little thing.
They don't need to know exactly what will happen every minute of the day.
They don't have all possible questions written down,
or the answers firmly established in their minds.
Teachers aren't in charge of all the thinking in the room.
They aren't the stars of the show.

Rather, they are the ones inviting students
to imagine, create, wonder, invent, and learn.

Teachers offer children the keys to the world
by initiating honest dialogue,
suggesting a search for alternatives,
prompting investigations.

No longer viewed as a sage on the stage,
the effective teacher is a guide on the side.
This shift in perception
profoundly changes the dynamics of interactions.
It activates genuine learning
as children own their involvement in the process.

Teachers trust and know that
as they compel questions to flow,
as they encourage higher levels of thinking,
and as they cultivate collaboration
among the students,
learning is the natural outcome.

Teachers facilitate this process,
posing thoughtful questions without known answers,
persuading students to make inferences and connections.

Children become independent thinkers,
masters of their education.
Authentic self-esteem flourishes.

Teachers are peace seekers

Teachers know children will sometimes feel discomfort,
unhappiness, or frustration
when life doesn't go a particular way.
Disagreements with others
are bound to happen.

The strength of a teacher lies in helping children
to truly see others as
precious human beings
who deserve to be treated with respect,
just as they would like to be treated.

The essential message of
respectfully considering others
is a foundation for students
as they develop their ability
to transform conflicts into peaceful resolutions.

Intuitive teachers model and encourage students
to listen and hear another's point of view,
to use words of compassion,
never words of hate,
as they work through a breakdown in communication.

With sensitivity and perceptive vision,
teachers guide children to become peace seekers
who are committed to a win-win solution for all.
A commitment like this has power.
A commitment like this can transform the world.

Teachers are confidence builders

Some children wear their worries,
like battered backpacks,
causing them to stumble and feel weary.

Nervous and hesitating,
they perceive school as just one more place to fail.
They tell themselves they are incapable,
that learning is for everyone else,
but not for them.
They are unwilling to take a risk.
For them, school isn't safe.

When students hear their inner doubting voice
constantly insisting
that something bad may happen,
that something may go wrong,
that someone will prove
they aren't good enough,
turmoil rules and learning suffers.

Worry and self-doubt is fear in disguise.
Fear of the unknown,
of not meeting someone else's standards of success.
And fear of the "what ifs?"

Helping students to practice reframing
their doubts and worries
into healthy and hopeful belief statements,
teachers empower students
to examine and eliminate their baseless fears,
and take a confident step forward.
One small step,
then another,
and another.

You are good enough!
You can learn!
You are perfectly imperfect,
and that's just exactly the way you are supposed to be!
You can do whatever you decide to do!
Anything is possible if you believe in yourself!

Children *can* learn
how to gain power over their own thinking
and reprogram doubtful internal messages.
By replacing negatives
with positive thoughts and actions,
children *can* hush the worrying dialogue,
eliminate the constant criticism,
conquer the fear.

With compassionate teachers at their sides,
students learn to think and act
in confident, purposeful ways.
They stand up straight,
breathe deeply,
move forward.
They take a chance.

Teachers are learners

The never-ending quest to learn more,
to explore more,
to become more,
is what sustains and invigorates a teacher.

Teaching certificates in hand,
some might think the teachers have completed
all the studying and learning they need.
But the real training has only just begun.

Teachers *never* want to stop learning,
or reading, or writing, or thinking.
They are constantly seeking new approaches
to improve their craft
and to inspire their students
on a grand journey of discovery.

Impassioned with curiosity, wonder,
and a need to understand things,
teachers surround themselves
with mentors, adventures,
and opportunities for enlightenment.
They fill up their minds with new ideas
and nurture themselves with glorious inspirations.

As they venture out with their class
on the treasure hunt for knowledge,
teachers radiate a love of learning.
Children absorb this energy like fresh air.

Teachers and their students grow,
feeling the exquisite joy of knowing a new thing,
and lighting up places that once were dark.

Learning feeds hungry minds, hearts, and souls.

Teachers are puzzle solvers

Reading, writing, 'rithmetic,
art, music, and gym,
teachable moments, reachable goals,
individual needs of children.

It appears to be a puzzle.
A myriad of seemingly disjointed bits and pieces.
All valuable.
And all deserving to be woven into a meaningful whole.

How do these elements really fit together?
How are they transformed
into a cohesive mosaic?

Teachers understand how to organize the jigsaw,
how to separate the really important
from the kinda important,
and concentrate on what's most important of all.

Thoughtfully combined academic and life lessons
allow children to move easily
from one experience to the next.
It makes sense to them.
A day arranged for maximum effectiveness
with just enough time for castle building.

It's a beautiful harmony.
And not so puzzling after all.

Teachers are singers

The teensy weensy spider never gave up.
Undaunted and looking forward to her brand new day,
the spider began working again,
forgetting all about the rain that washed her web away.

Life lessons quietly take root in hearts
as children sing simple songs with their teachers and friends.

If an *ant can move a rubber tree plant*
just by having high hopes,
imagine what can happen when a child sets his or her mind
to a seemingly difficult challenge.

And remembering to *make new friends, but keep the old*
is grand advice
as children practice the skill of getting along in the world.

Age-old wisdom and universal truths show up
in the early songs of school.

Teachers *merrily, merrily, merrily, merrily*
encourage positive visualizations with the notion
that *life is but a dream.*
They encourage children to dream big dreams.

In the elegance of school songs,
we honor *America's purple mountain majesties,*
and memorize our ABCs.

From the silly to the serious, traditional to patriotic,
music has the amazing capacity
to remind us about the important things in life.

Leading an exuberant choir of voices, joyfully, loudly,
and a little off key,
teachers connect generation to generation.

Teachers are readers, seekers of knowledge

How did the ancient ones envision a pyramid?
Will we discover life in a far-off galaxy?
What can be done to save the endangered gorillas,
elephants, tigers, and whales,
and all of our planet's vanishing creatures?
Is a double rainbow especially enchanted?

Teachers and their students explore earthly secrets,
transport themselves back in time,
and propel themselves into the future
as they enter the kingdom of books.

Poets, dreamers,
keepers of legends,
we are drawn to their knowledge.
Their brilliance quenches a thirst,
felt even by the very young.

Reading evokes wondrous images,
opens doors to unexplored worlds,
and invites curious minds to seek answers
to the mysteries of the universe.

We read to notice life's littlest moments,
and to learn lessons from those who have come before us.
We can avoid mistakes of the past.
We can be authors of a brand new future.

Illumination is power.
Reading unifies our human spirit.

Teachers are wizards

Inside every teacher a wizard resides.
Sparkling and brilliant,
this luminescent spirit knows how
to speak to the young.

Concocting magic each and every day
with a dazzling dash of determination,
a succulent supply of spontaneity,
and an incandescent pinch of imagination,
teachers inspire brilliance
from their students
in effervescent explosions!

In the enchanted land where learning lives,
students are captivated
and mesmerized.

Some teachers actually sparkle and shimmer.
Others travel light years while standing quite still.
And some quietly foster astonishing feats from their students
with carefully chosen questions
intended to elicit deep thinking
or breathtaking actions.

Are these wizards in teacher's clothing,
or are the teachers employing wizardly enchantments?

It's a secret,
but it's obvious that spells are cast,
dreams are awakened,
and children achieve wisdom.

Teachers are dreamers, visualizers, imaginers

Infinite possibilities exist as teachers
invite their students
to imagine a healthier planet,
to envision lasting peace,
to embrace Martin's Dream.

Children begin to visualize dazzling answers
to mysterious questions.
They look ahead with hope.
Dreams are within reach.

Teachers know the world awaits idealists
who look to the future with
unconventional inventions,
awakened solutions,
and original thought.
In fact, the future depends
on thinkers with creative vision.

Insightful teachers cultivate conversations
that play with all ideas,
outrageous, fanciful, surprising, and profound.

Knowing their world is one of immeasurable abundance,
children glimpse the possible,
pursue the impossible,
and celebrate what can be.

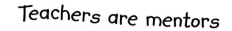

Teachers are mentors

A connecting thread runs through those who teach.
They share a desire to live a purposeful existence,
to work with others in a helpful role.
It is a way of living, a way of being.

And they never, ever feel done.
They think about their students on the way home,
while eating dinner,
while relaxing on the weekends,
even when they dream at night.

Students are carried around in their pockets,
they show up in their memories,
they tug at their heartstrings.

It's that connection,
that relationship, that bond,
that makes this profession more than a job.
Teachers have a rare opportunity
to assist a child
in reaching their highest potential.
It truly is a chance to make a difference in the world,
one child at a time.

Mentors listen to their hearts,
make insightful observations,
and change lives through personal connections.
With determination to do whatever can be done
to help their student achieve success,
the partnership is a strong one.

Teachers optimistically propose the challenge:
what would you attempt to do
if you knew you could not fail?

With relentlessly positive encouragement,
teachers empower their students
to choose wisely,
dream deeply,
imagine wildly.

Wondrous events unfold
as teachers awaken young minds
to the belief that everything is possible,
and they can
do anything,
anything,
anything!

Who are teachers?

Teachers are ordinary people
doing extraordinary acts,
sometimes so small
they may go unnoticed by anyone,
except one small child,
to whom that act
mattered immensely...

... and that is why we teach.